BIG LETTER TRACING
Workbook For Kids

By

Little Scholars Publishing

{THIS BELONGS TO:}

_____

_____

FREE Printable Worksheets for Preschool and Kindergarten Students

If you're seeking some more resources to aid in your child's learning journey, we have a selection of free printable worksheets available for preschool and kindergarten students. These worksheets are designed to help children develop their fine motor skills through tracing simple lines, curves, circles and shapes. This is an important precursor to learning how to write letters and numbers.

My selection of worksheets includes a variety of activities that are both educational and fun for children, and can be used at home, in the classroom, or as part of a homeschool curriculum. They are 100% FREE to download and print, and are easily accessible by scanning the QR code below.

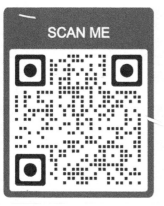

Regards,

Anastasia Stephen

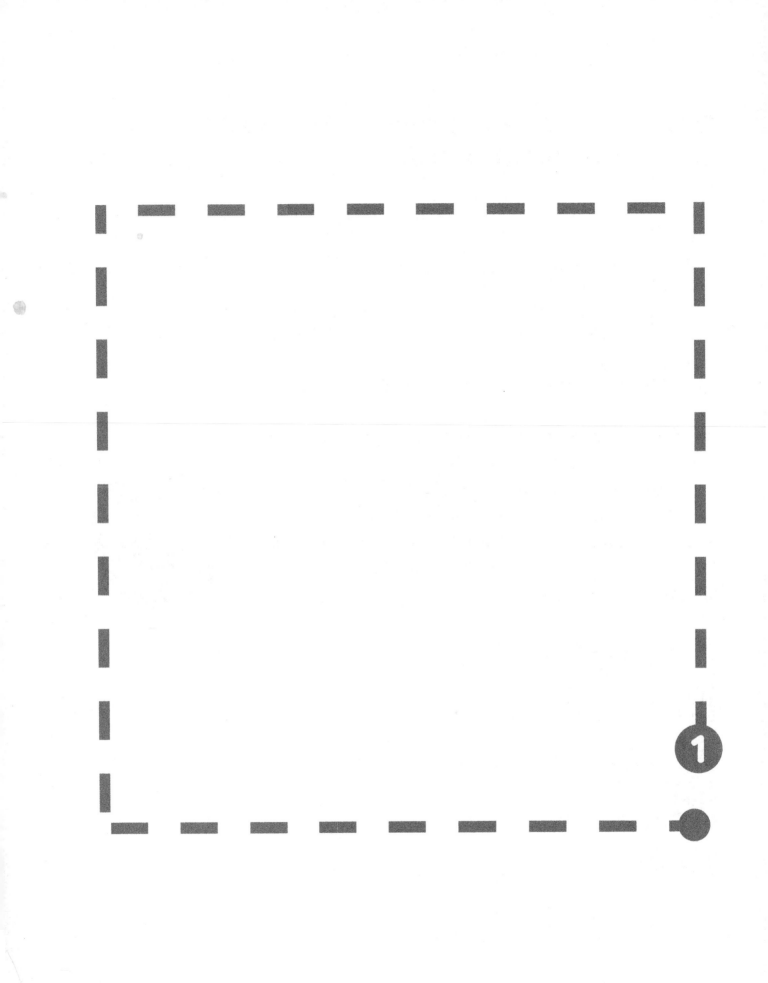

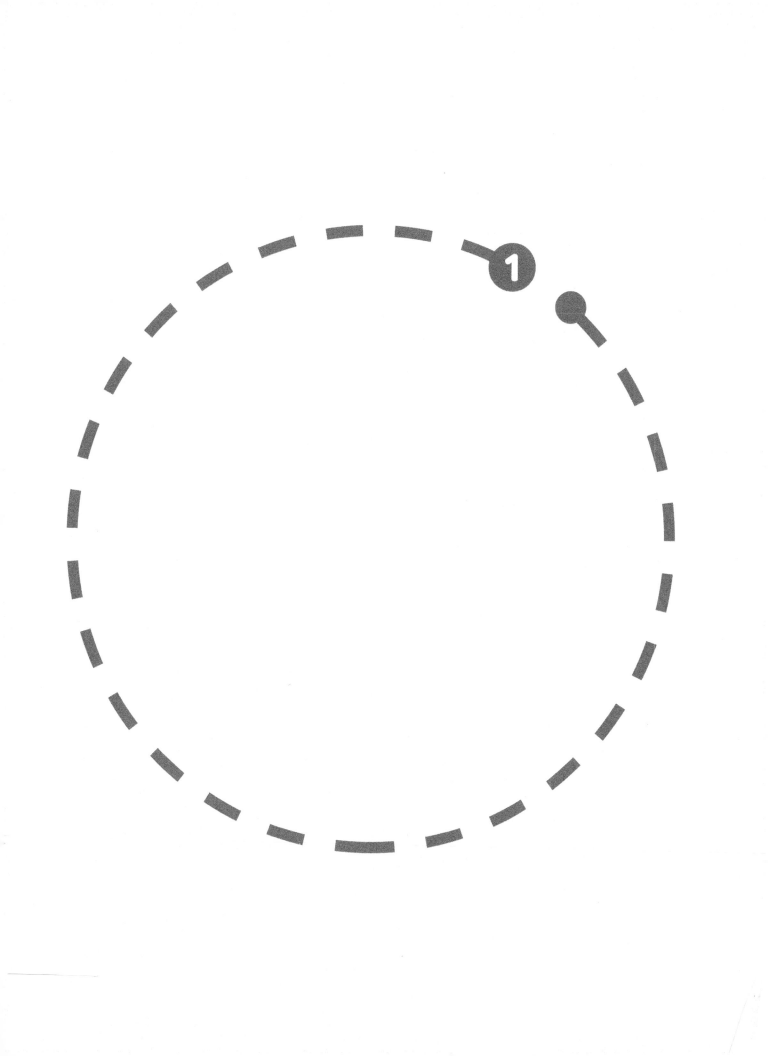

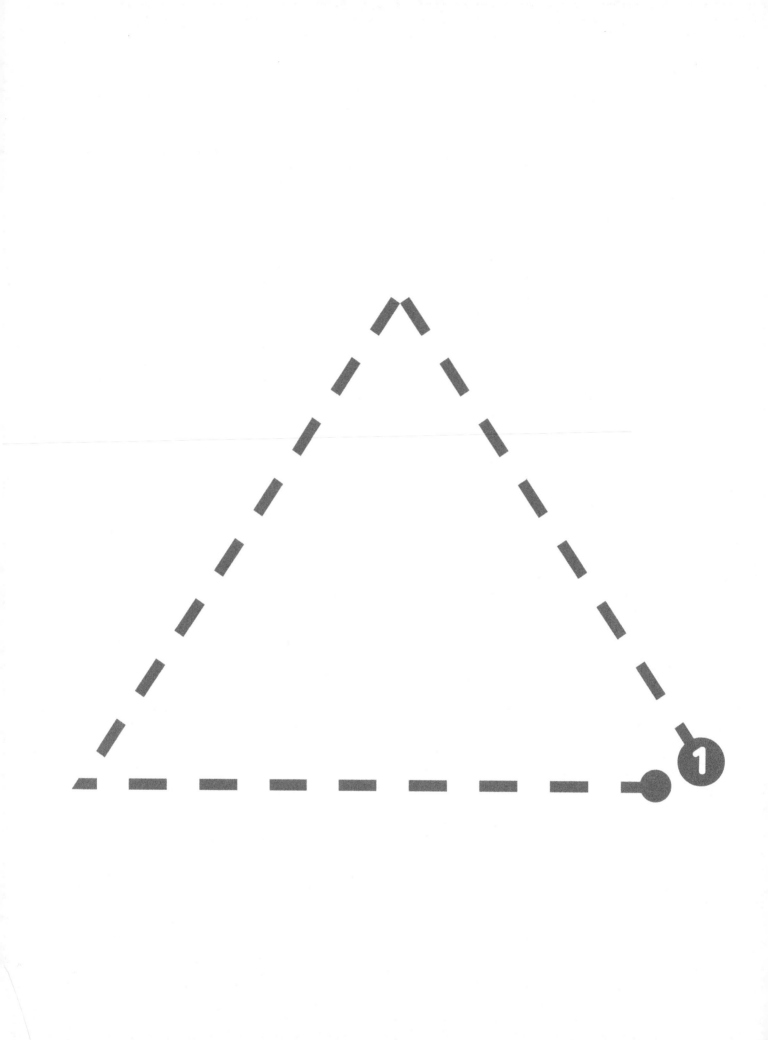

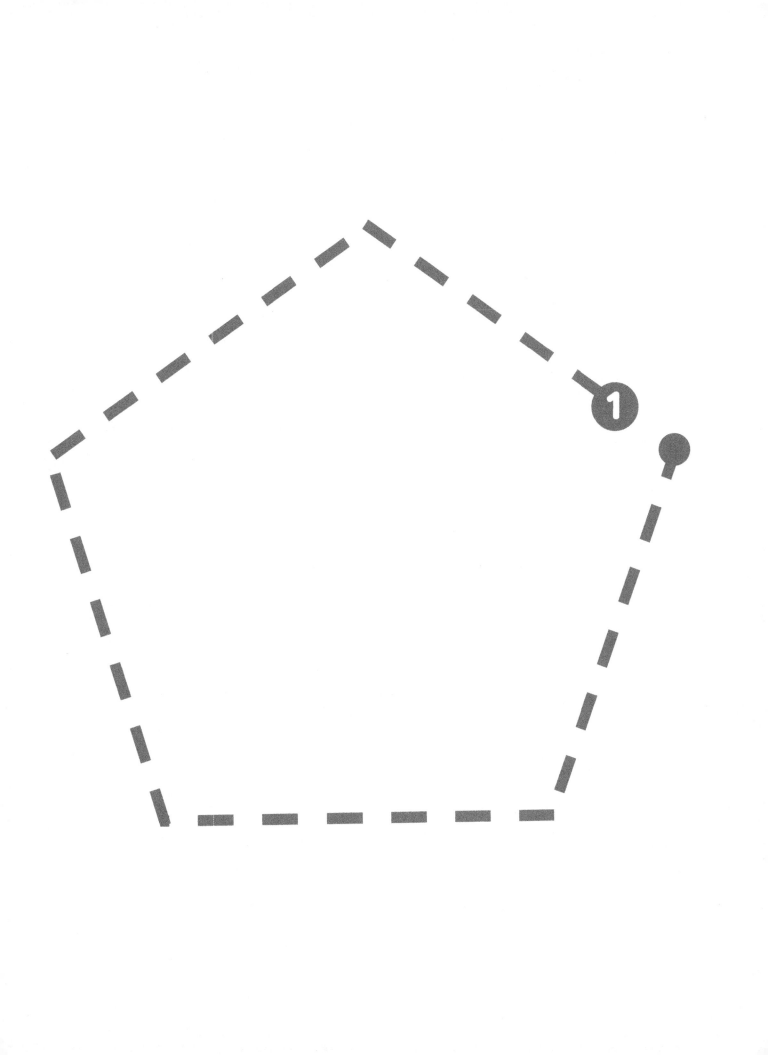

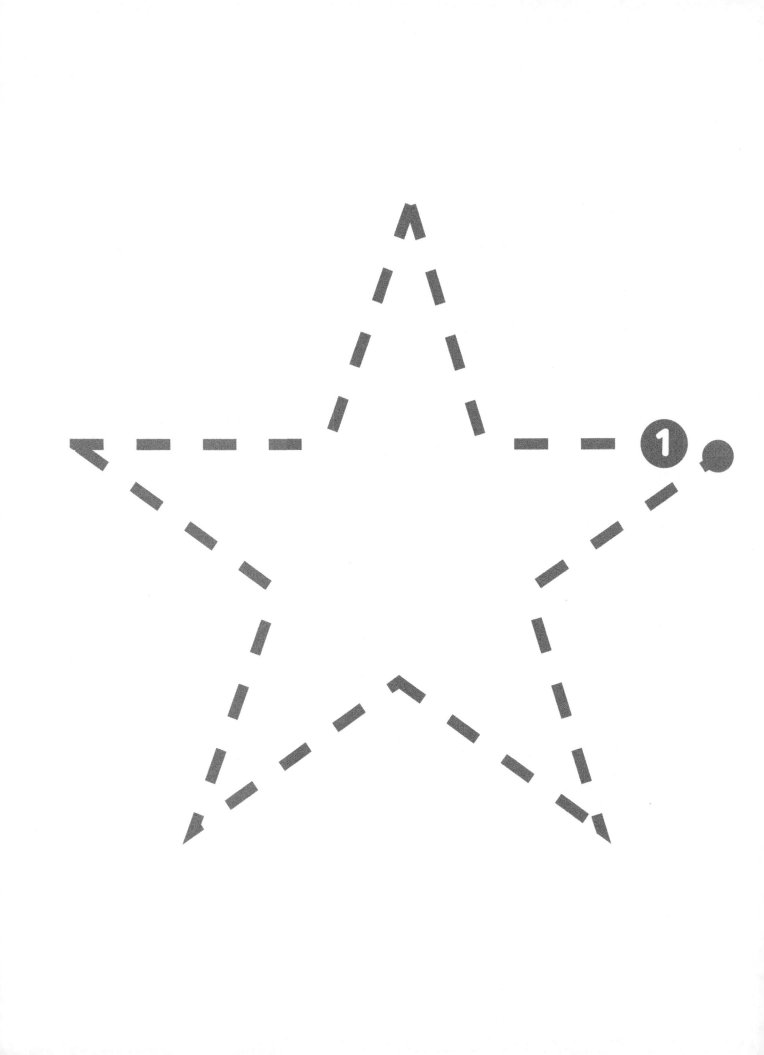

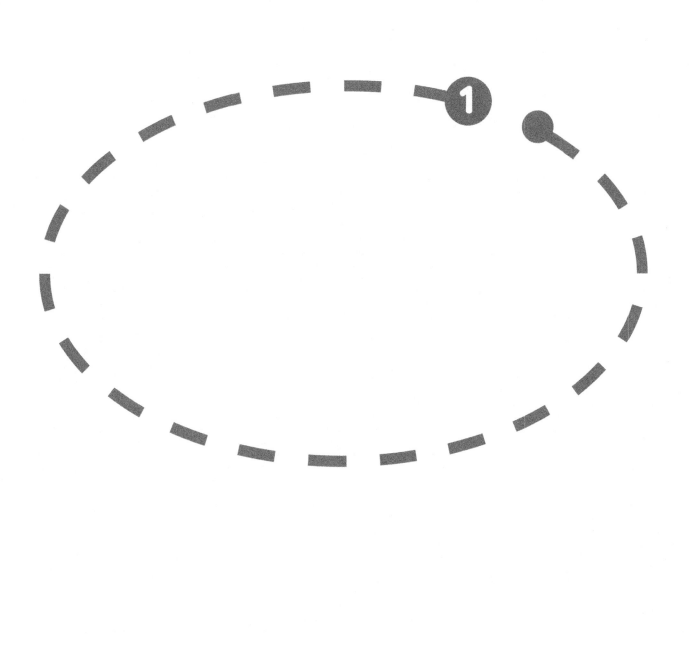

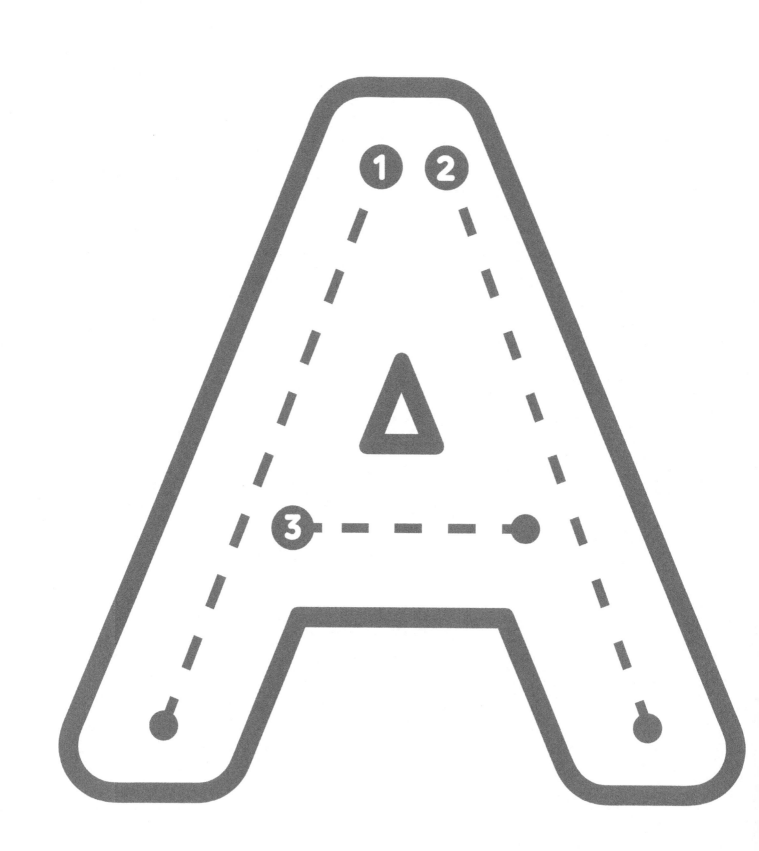

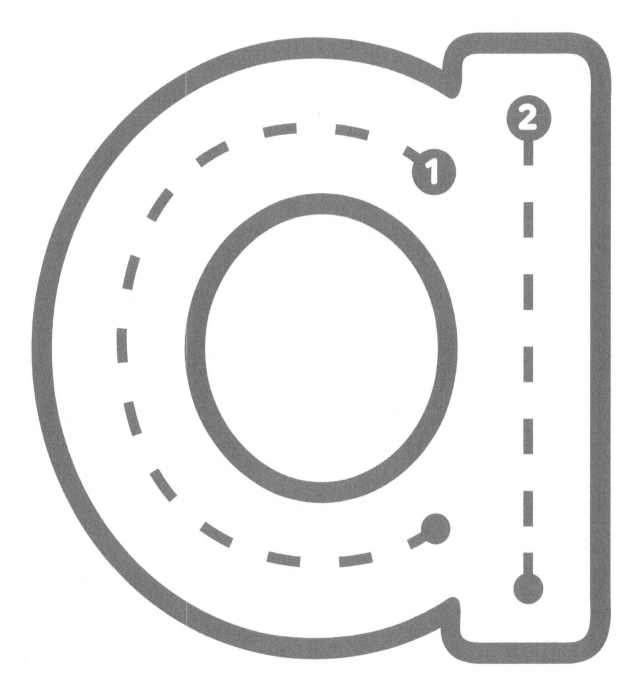

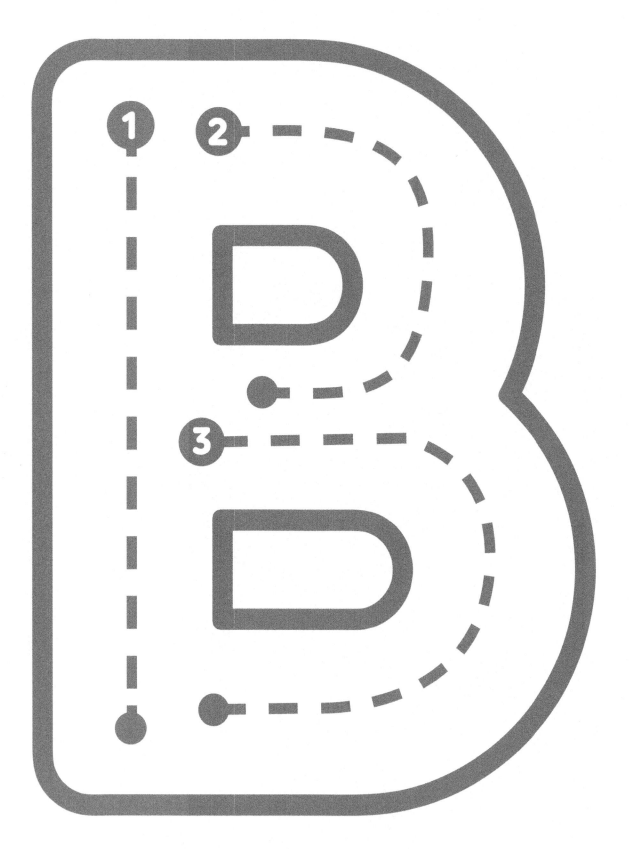

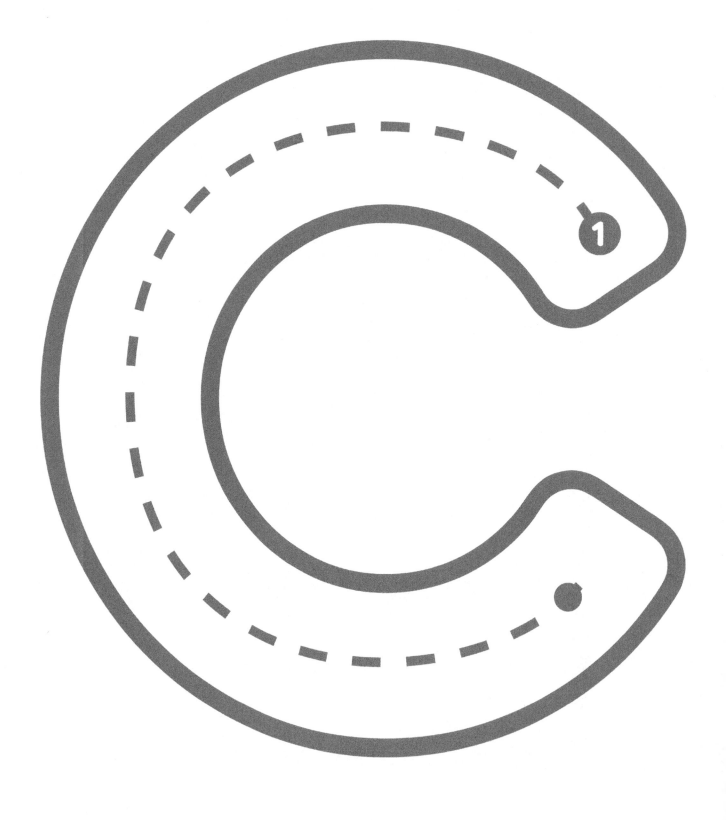

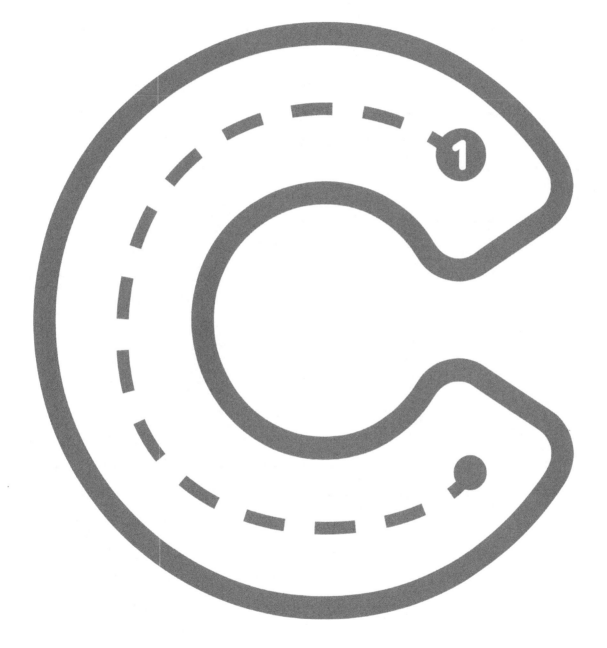

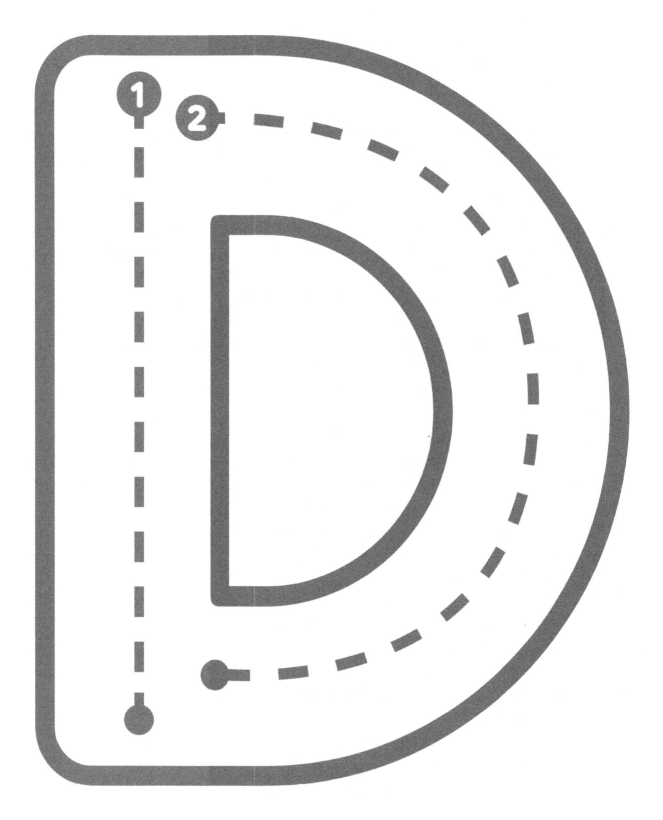

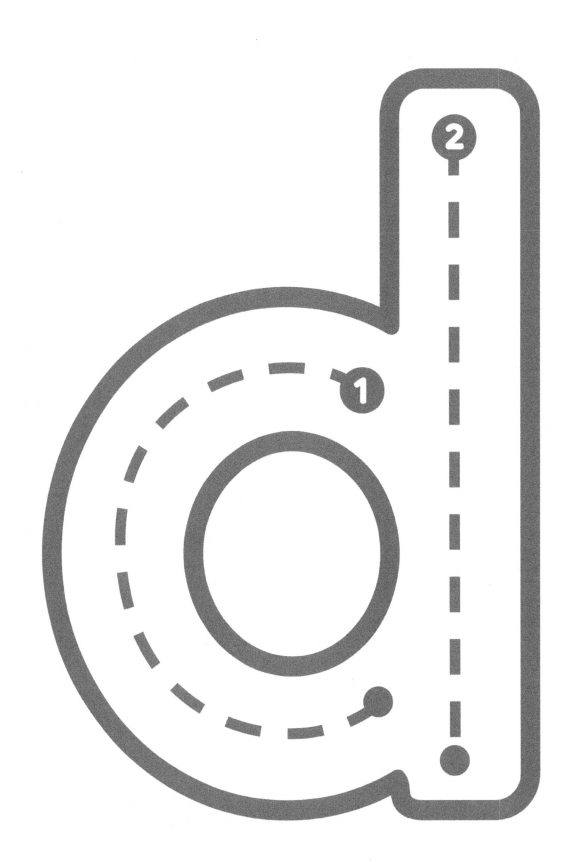

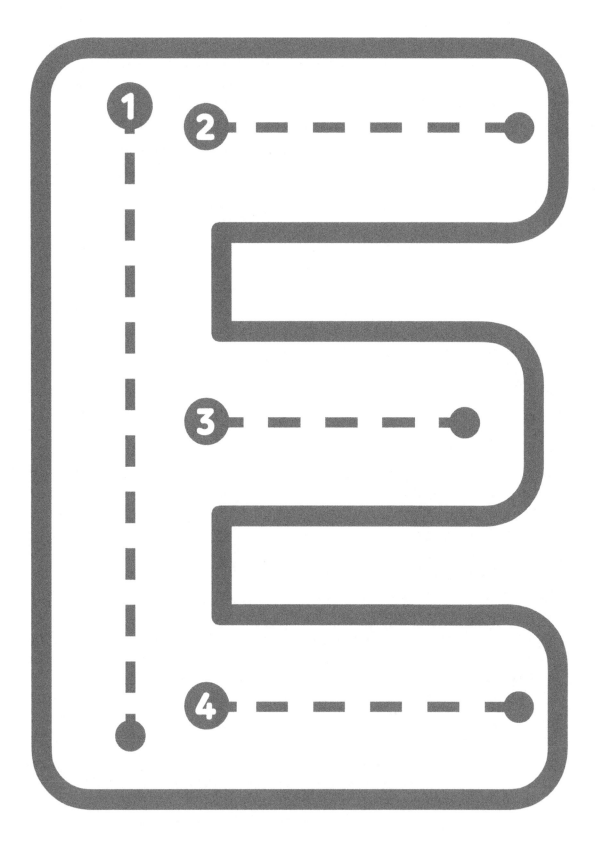

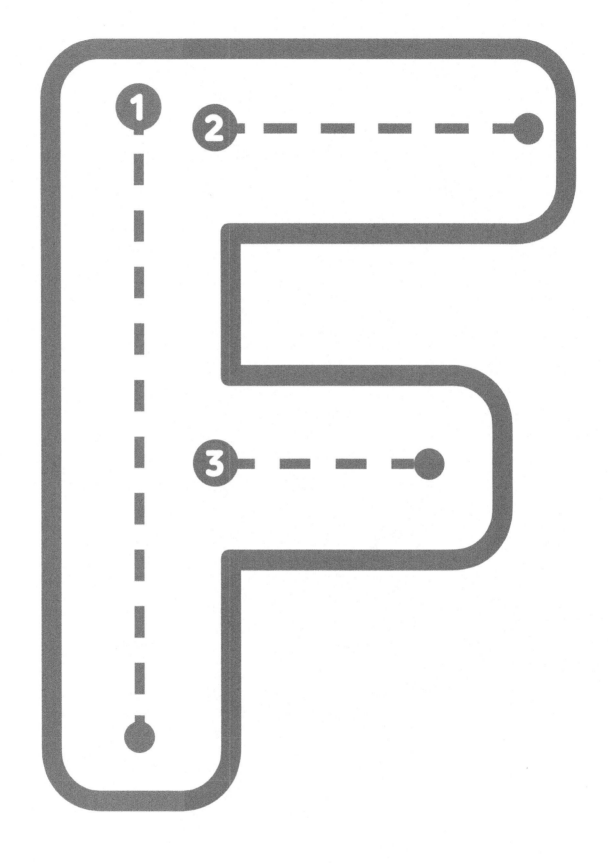

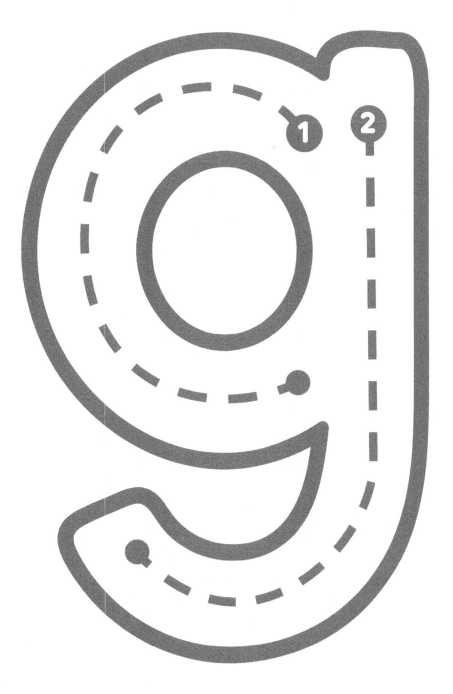

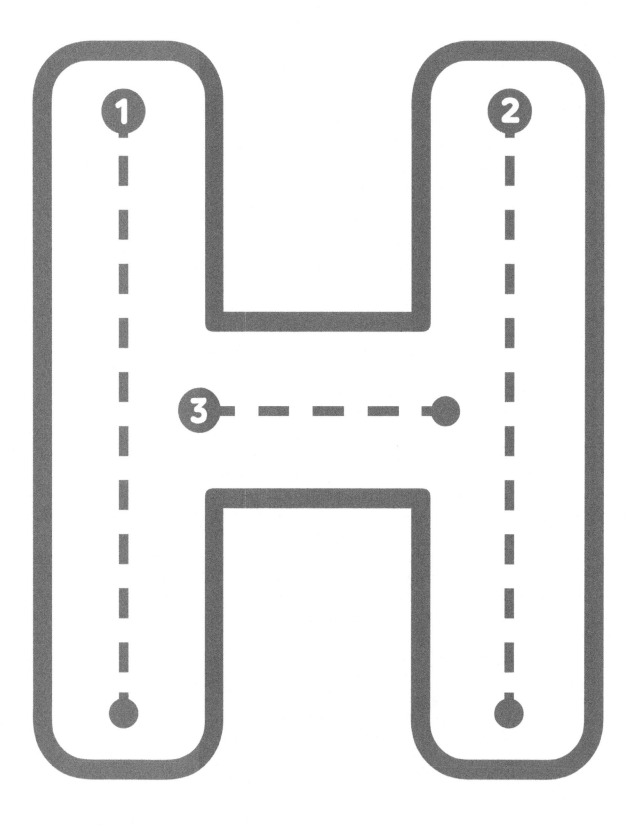

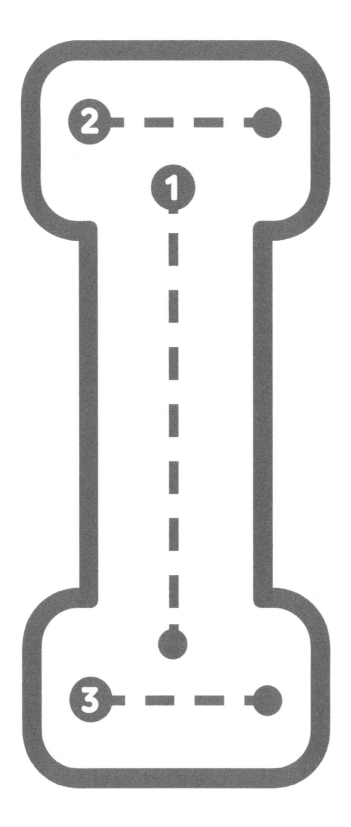

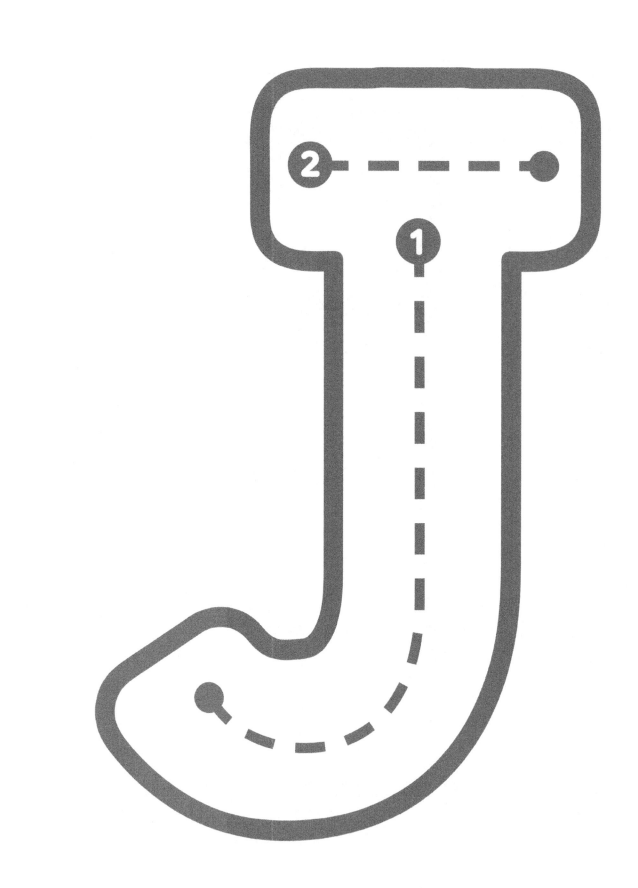

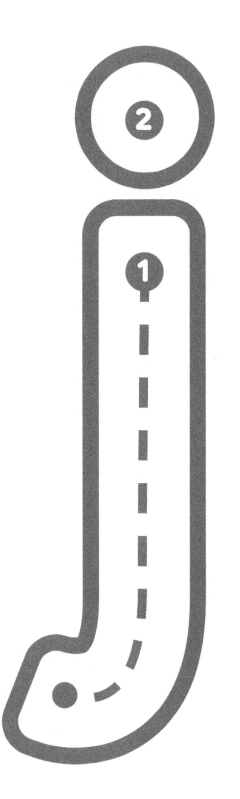

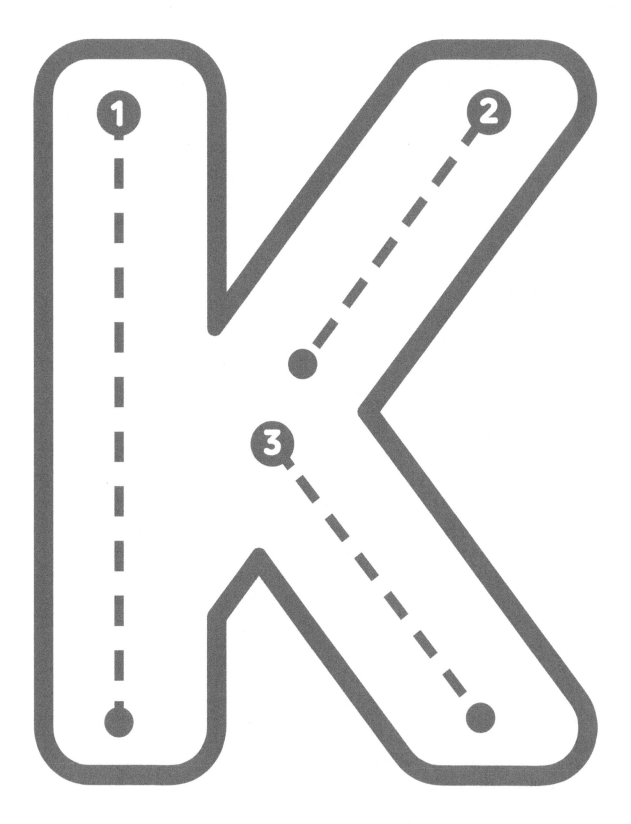

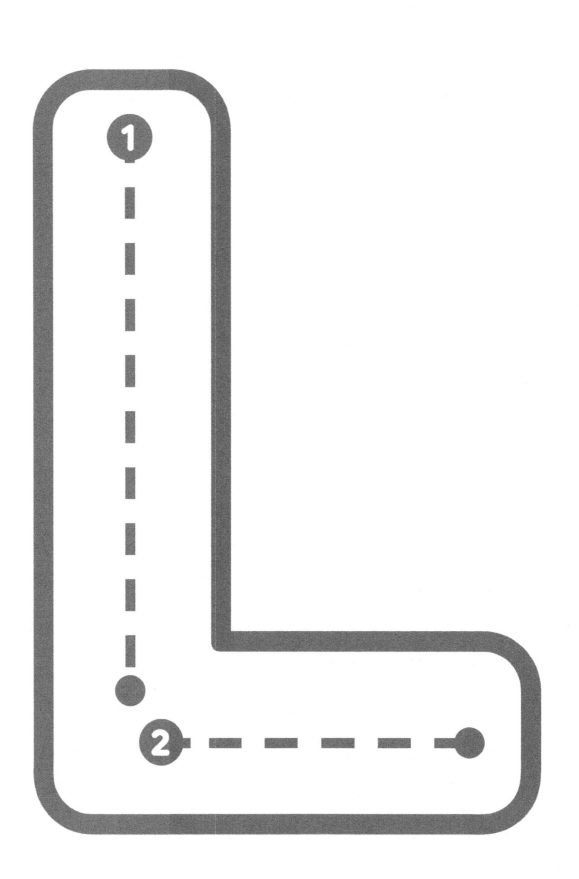

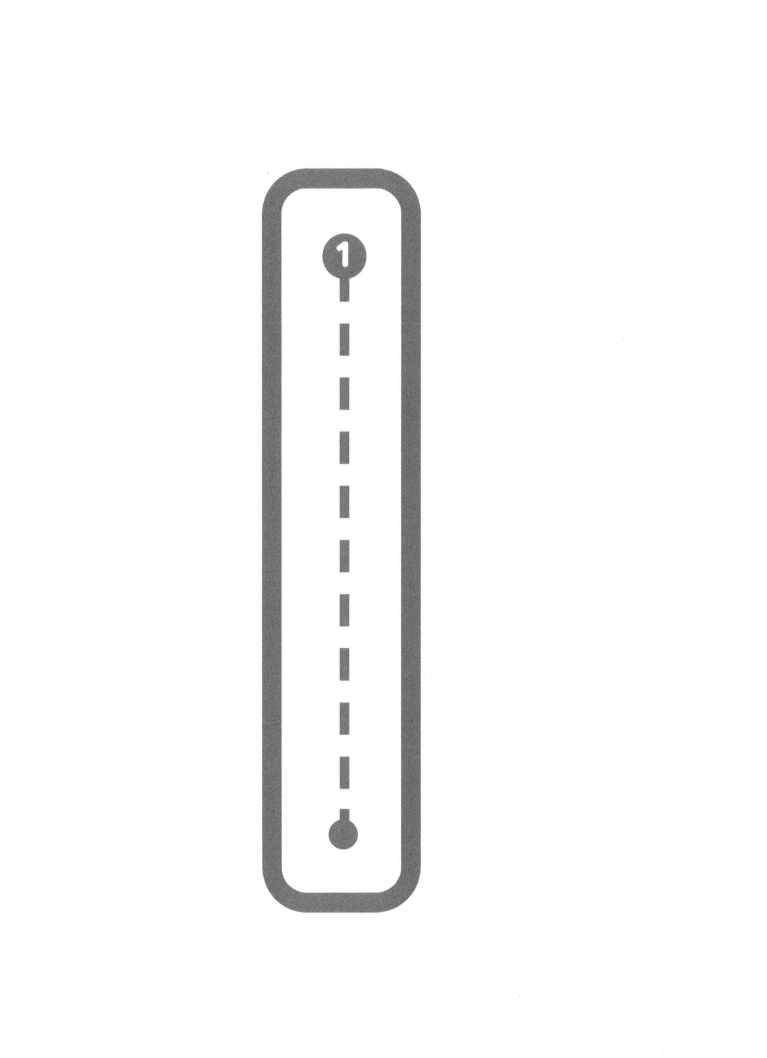

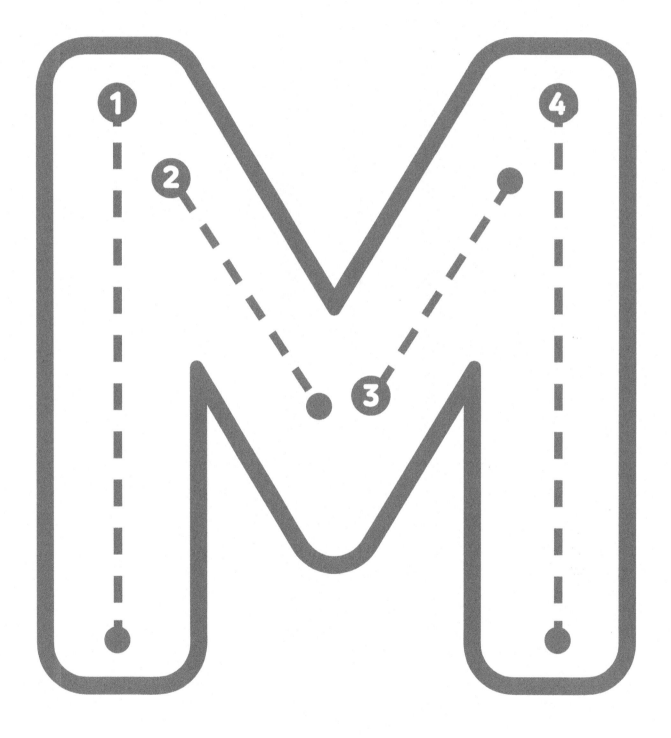

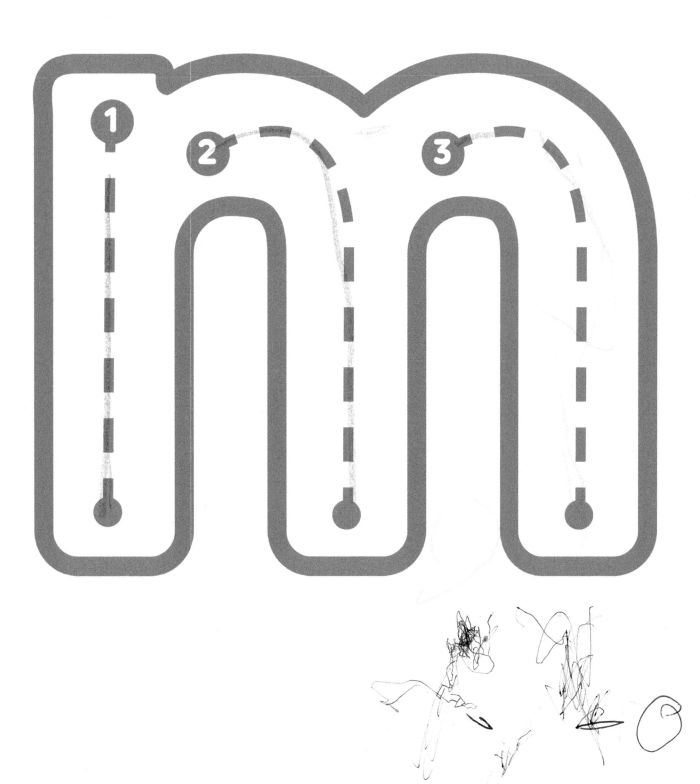

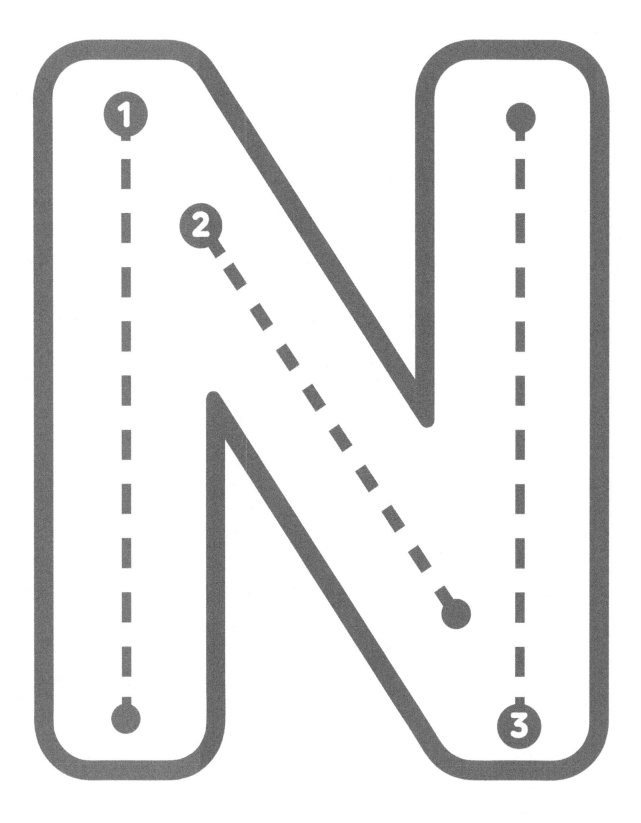

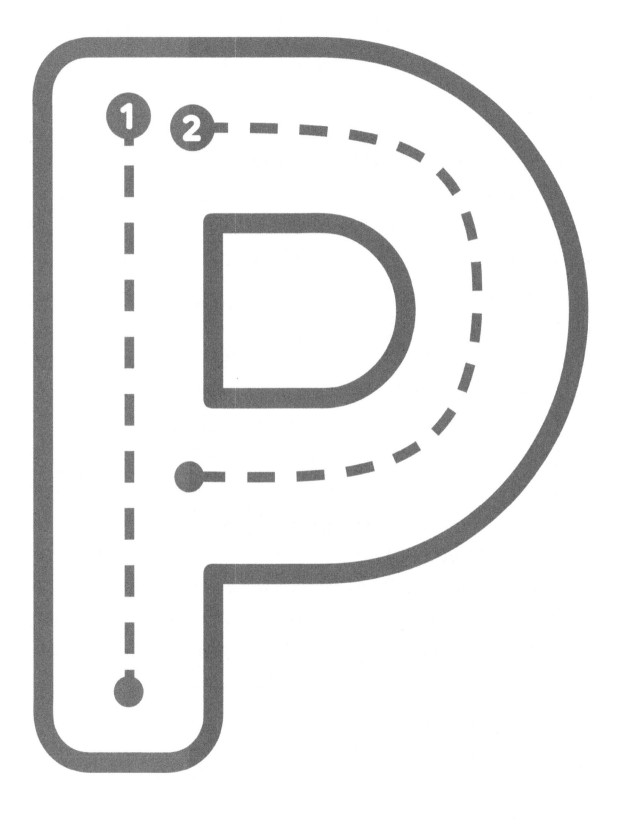

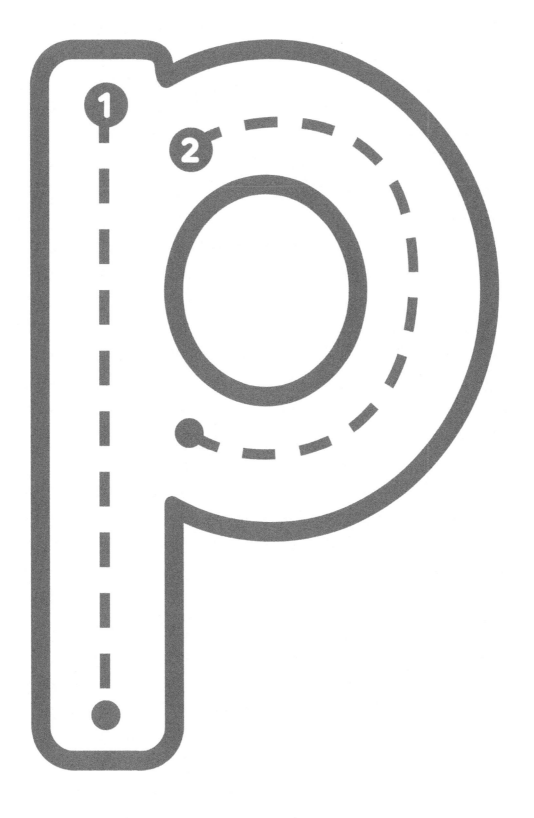

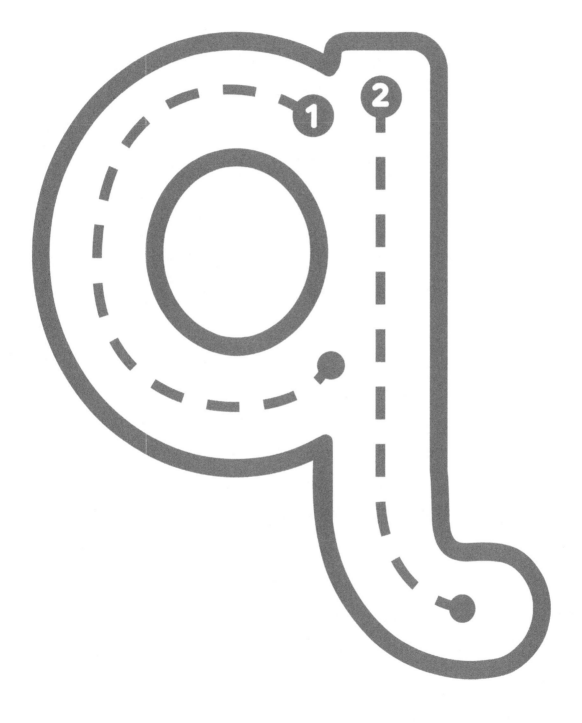

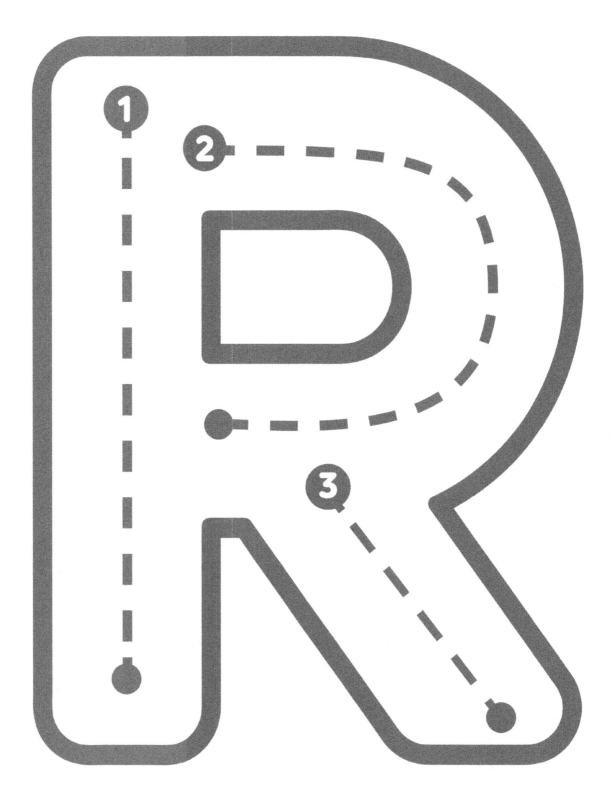

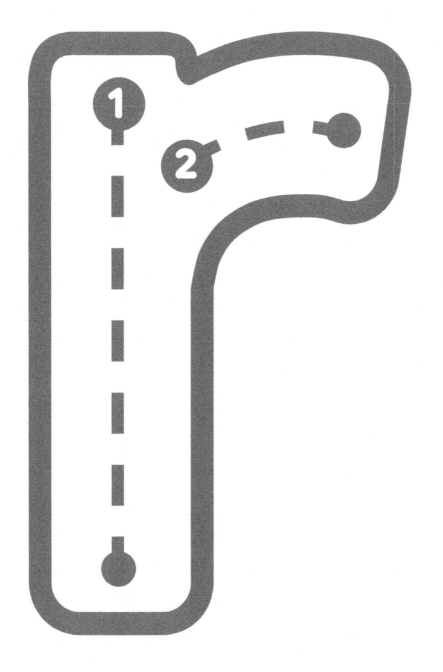

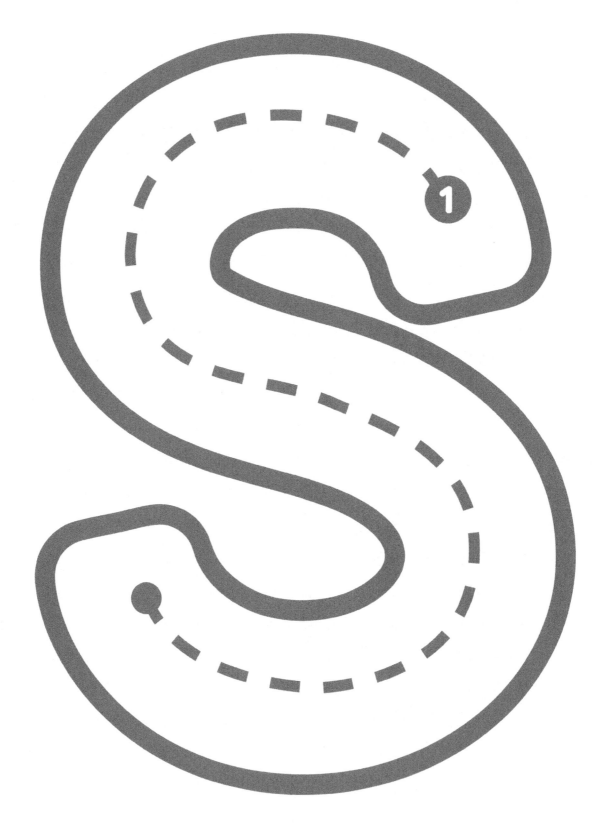

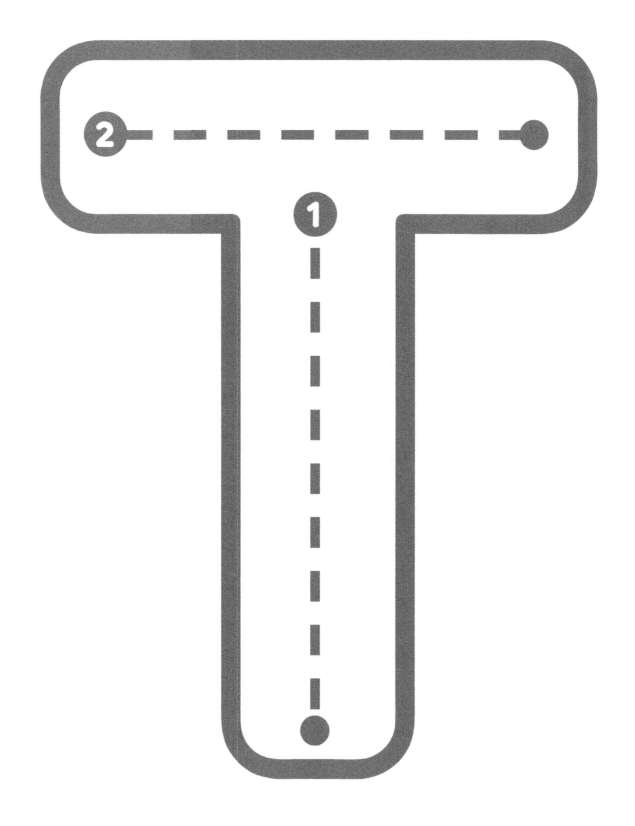

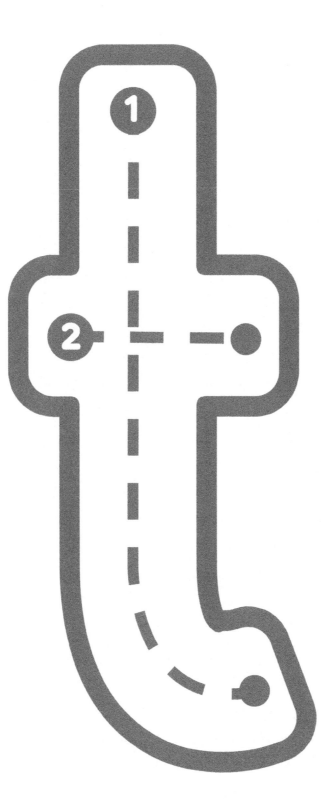

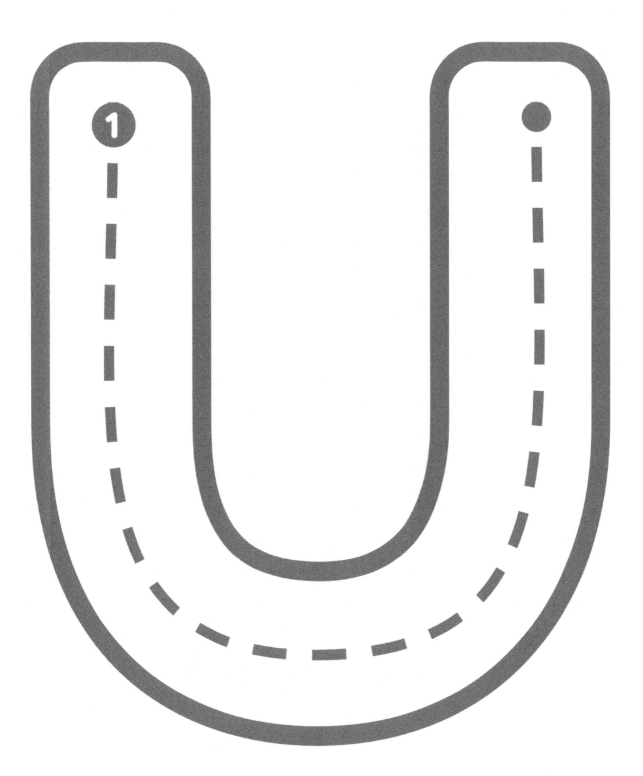

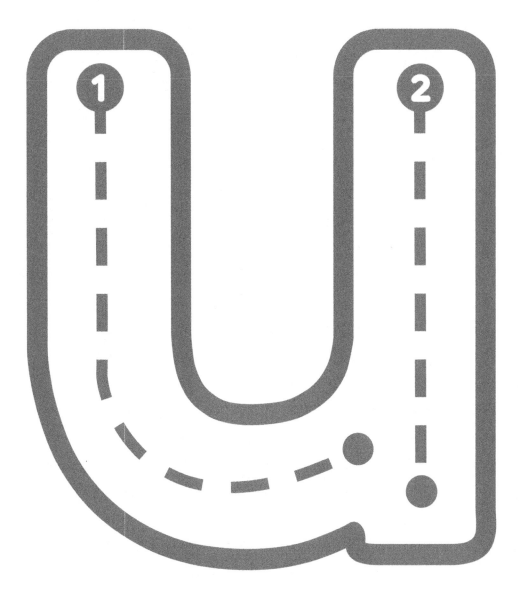

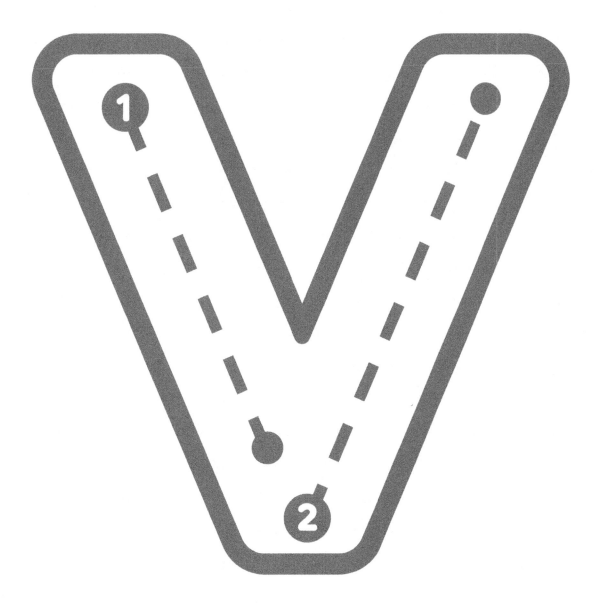

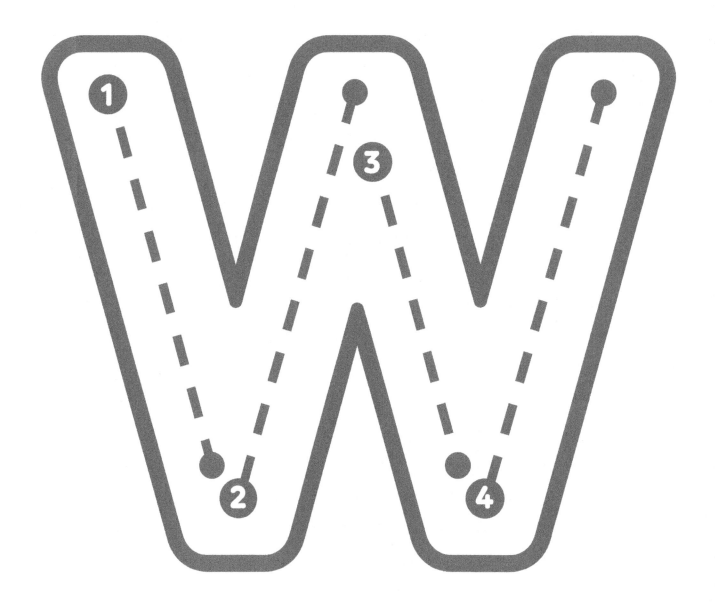

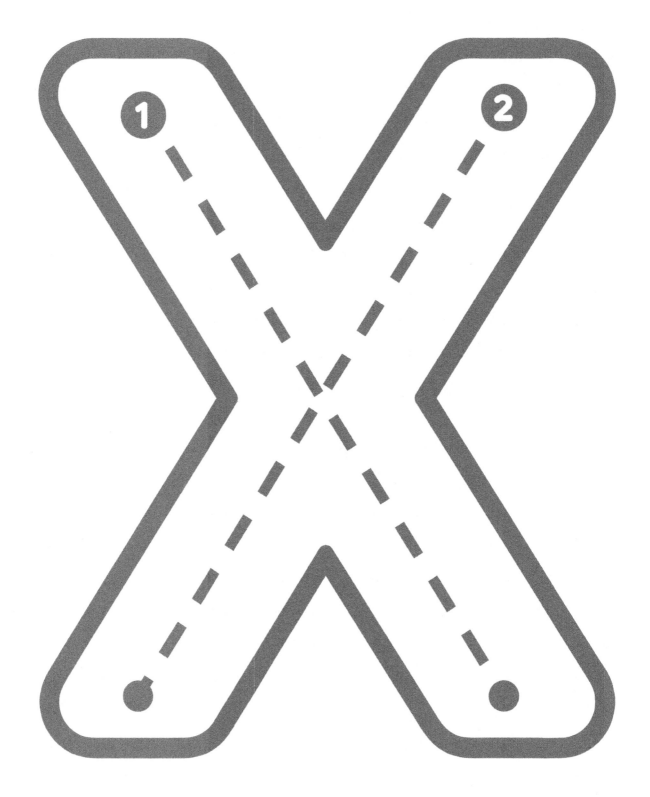

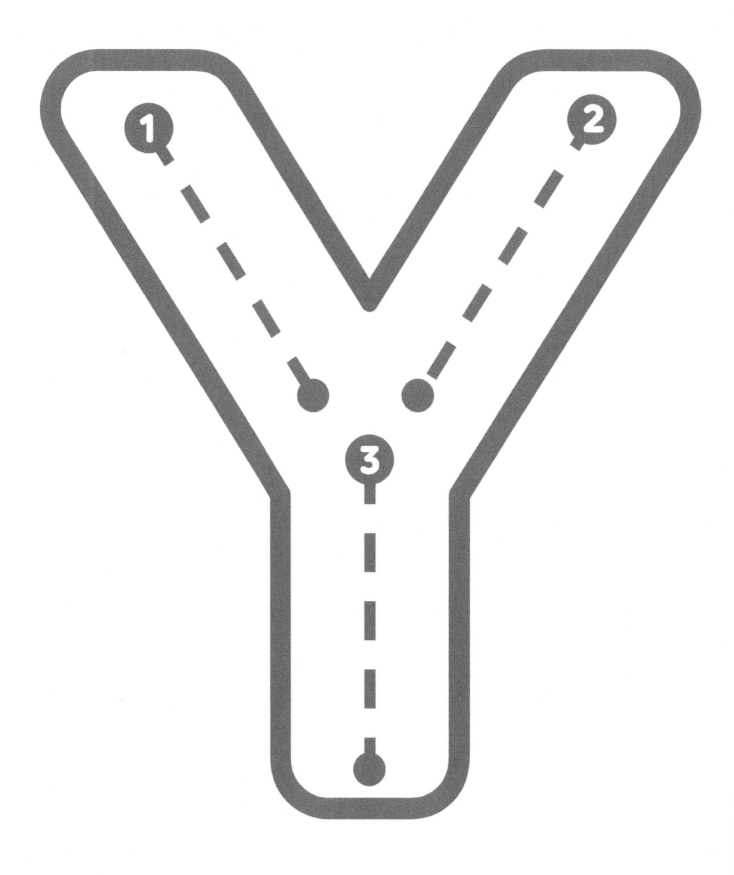

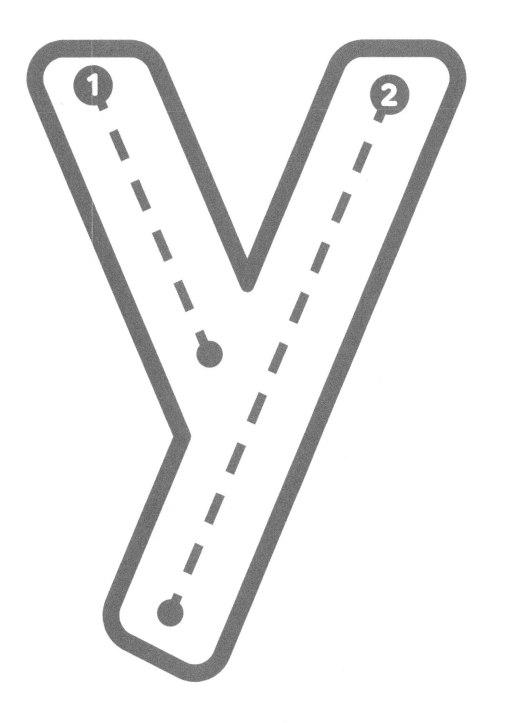

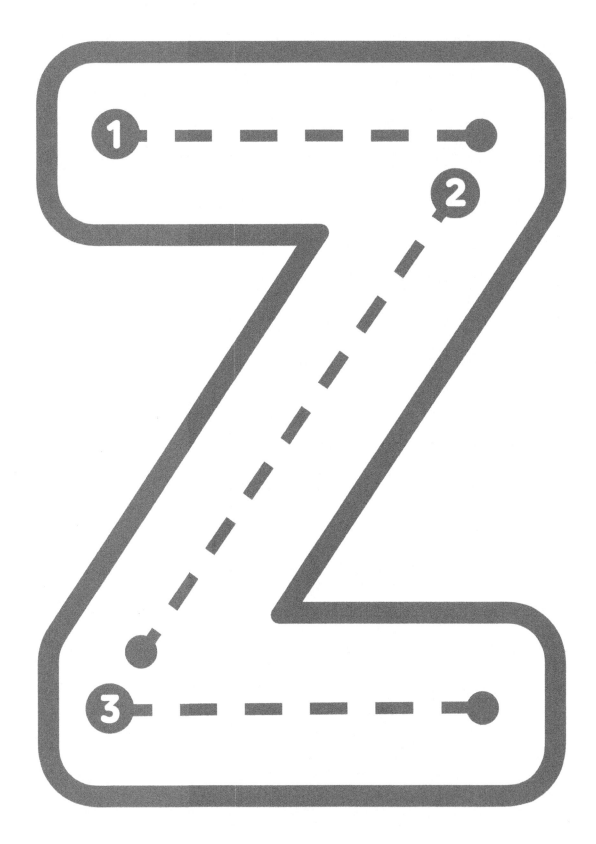

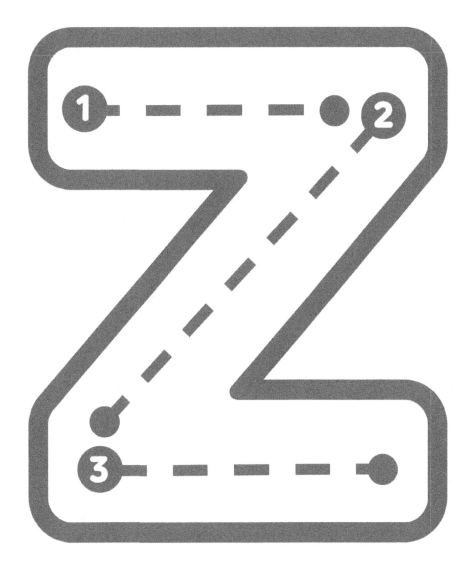

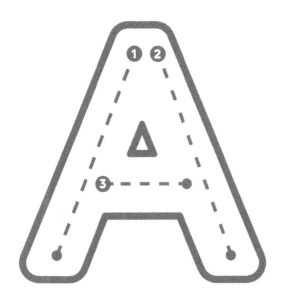
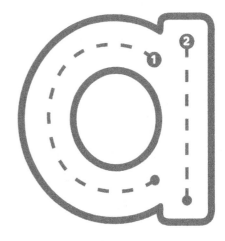
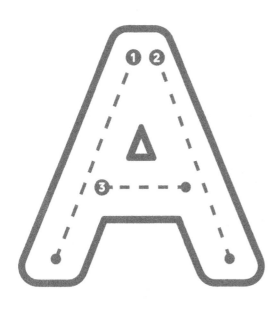
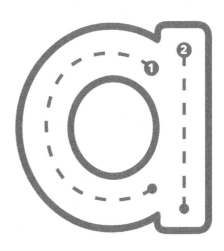
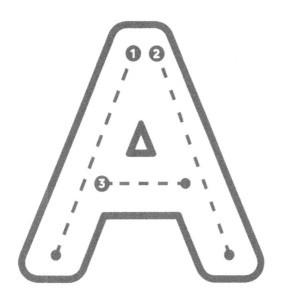
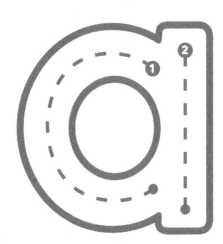

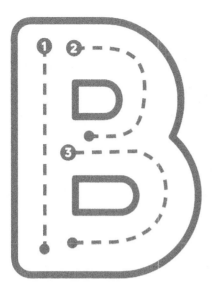

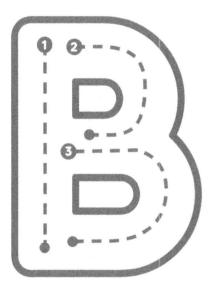

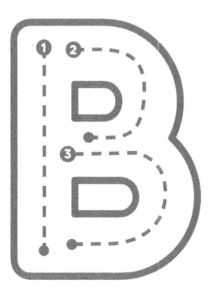

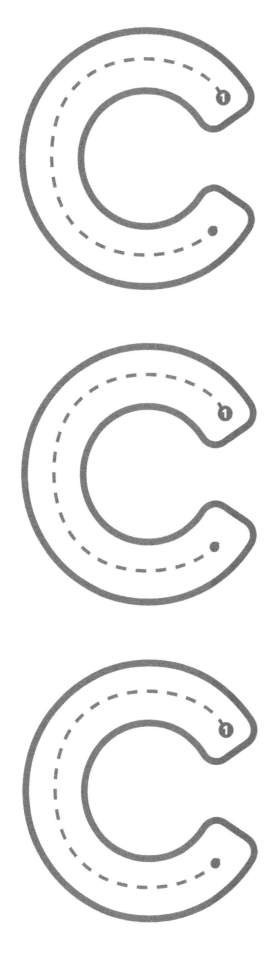
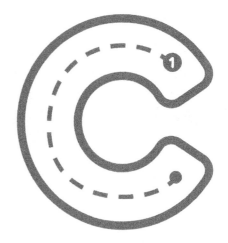
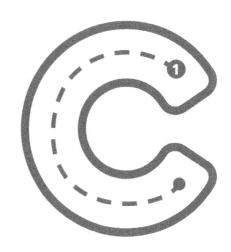
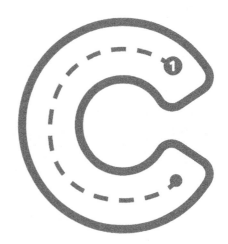

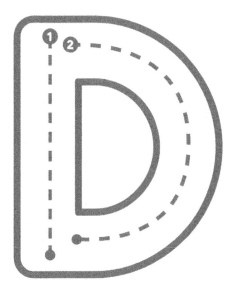
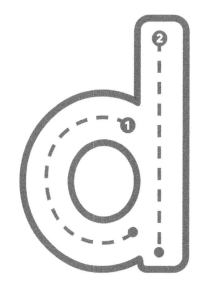
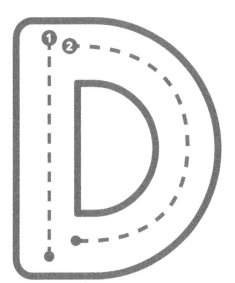
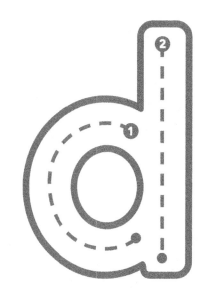
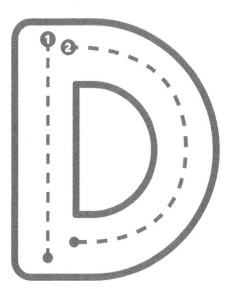
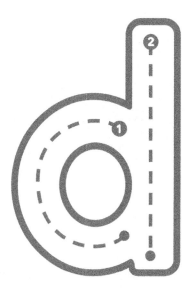

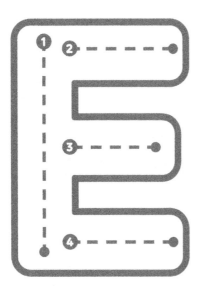

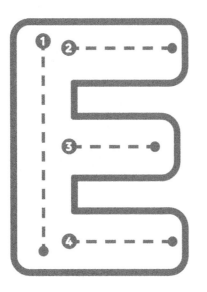

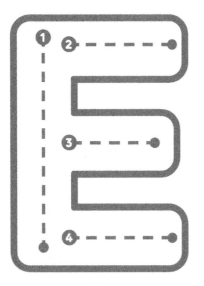

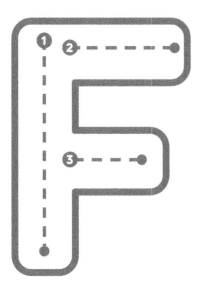

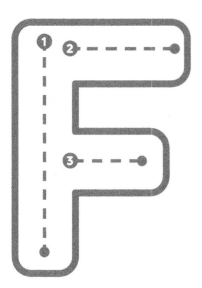

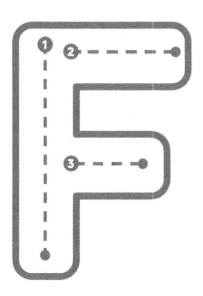

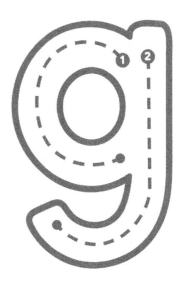

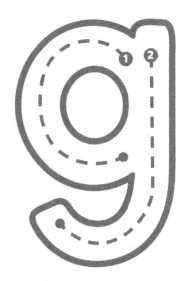

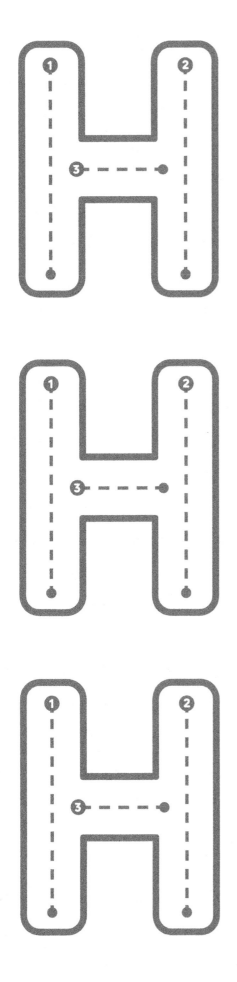

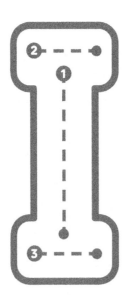

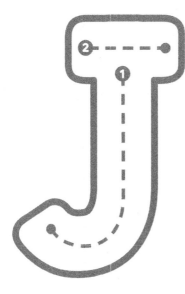 

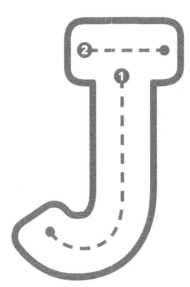 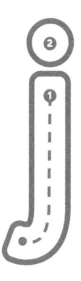

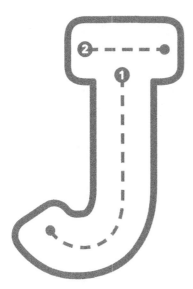 

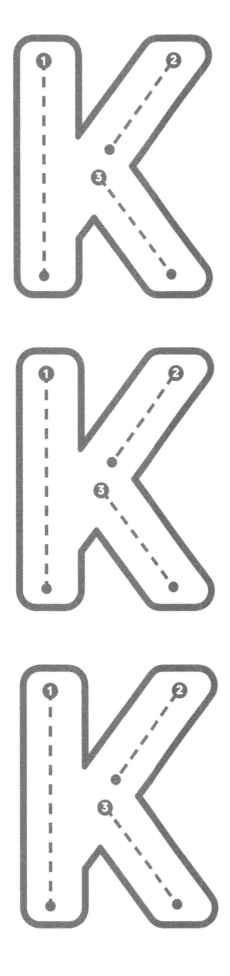
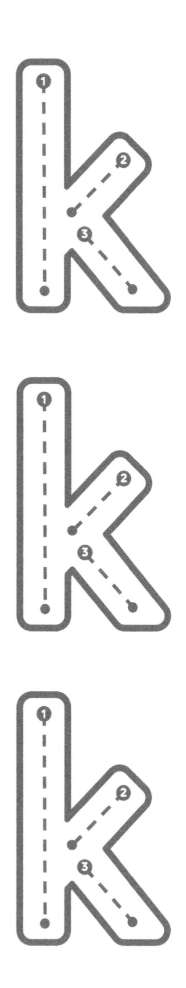

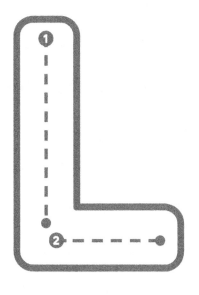

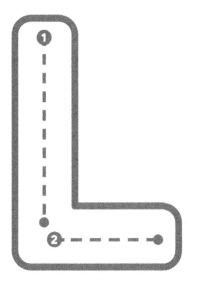

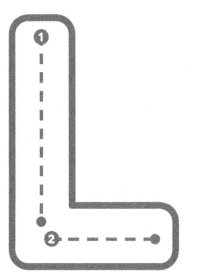

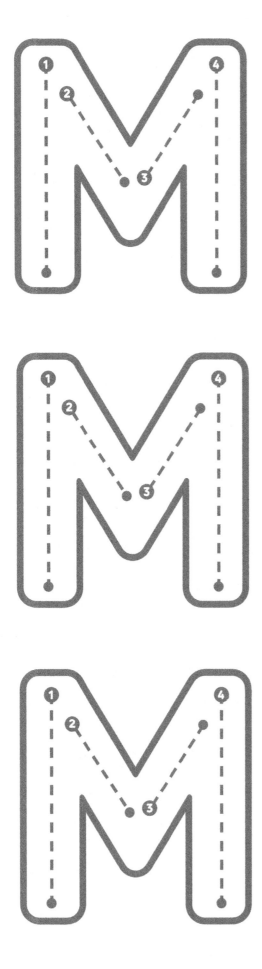
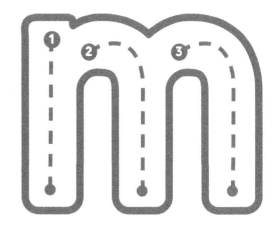
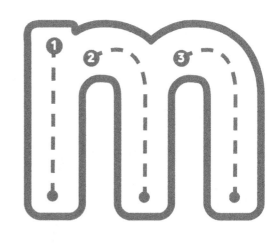
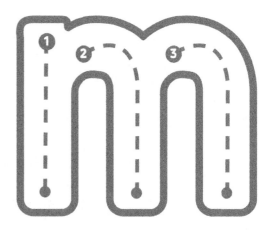

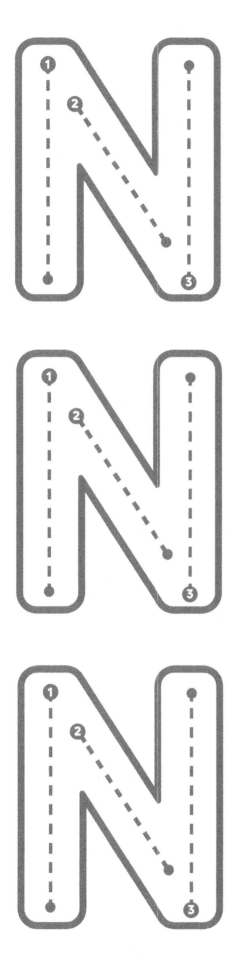
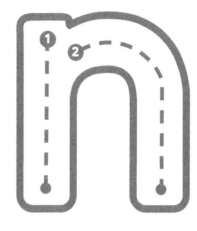
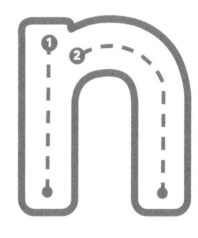
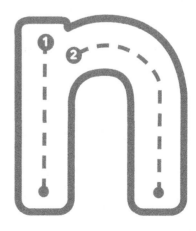

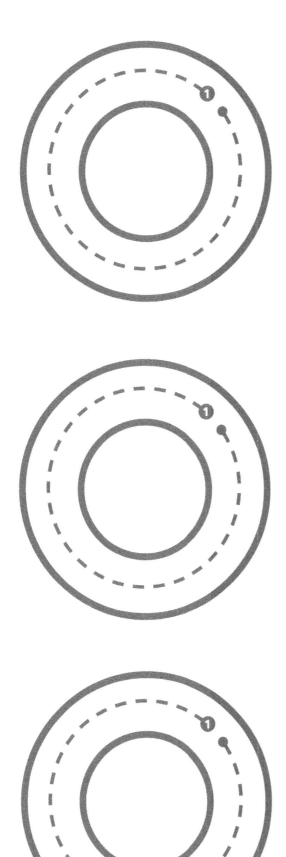

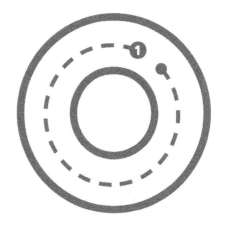

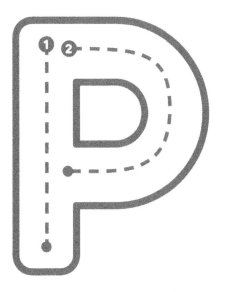
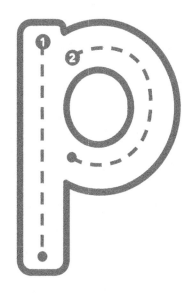
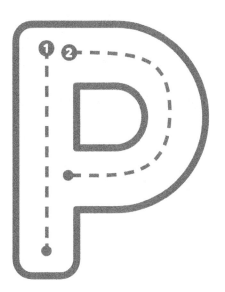
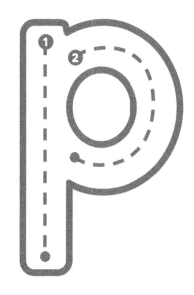
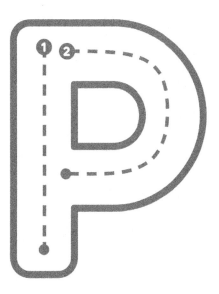
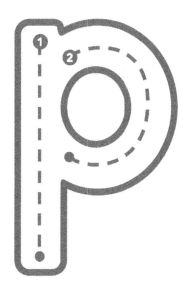

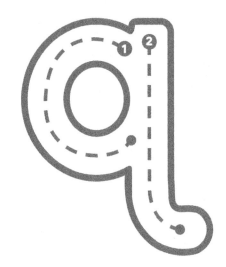

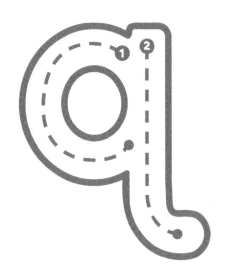

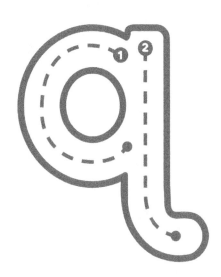

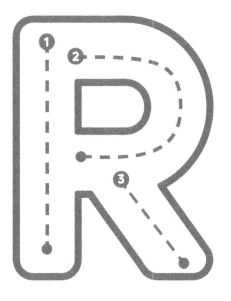
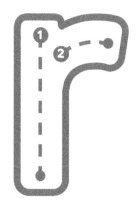
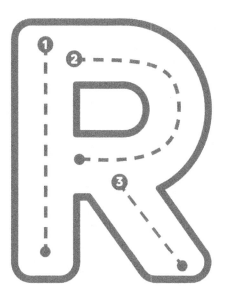
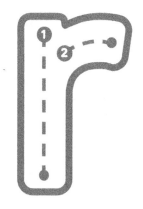
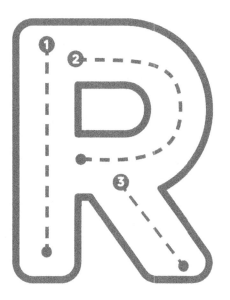
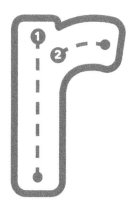

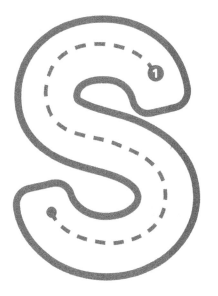

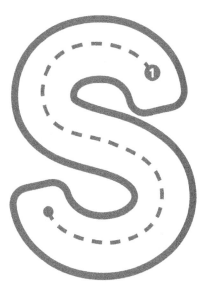

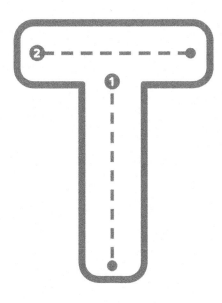
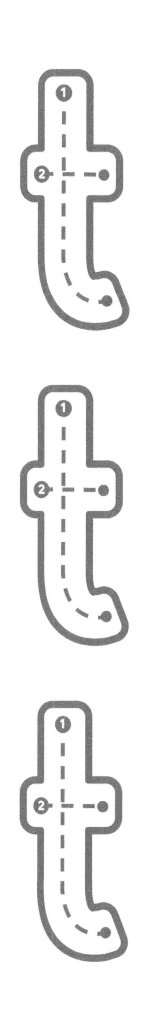
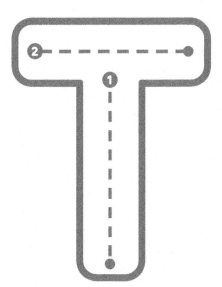
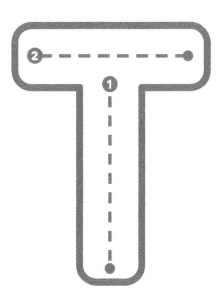

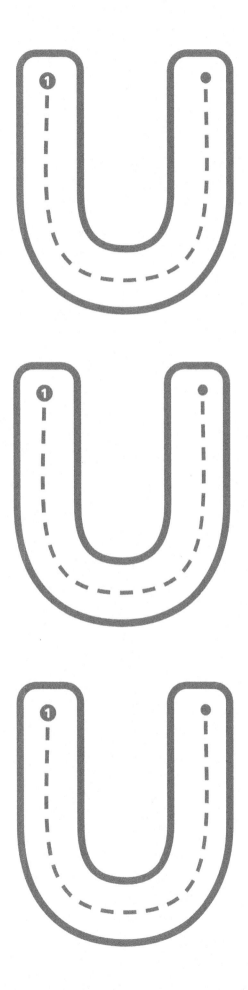
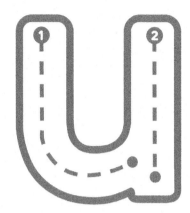
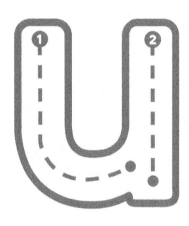
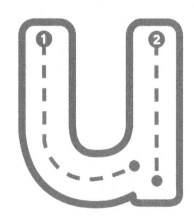

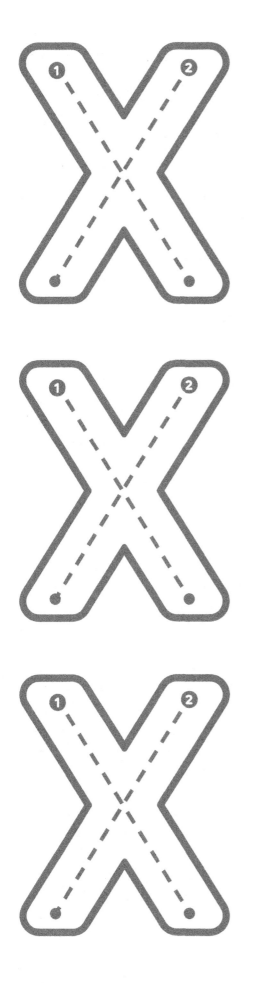

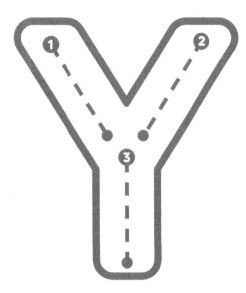
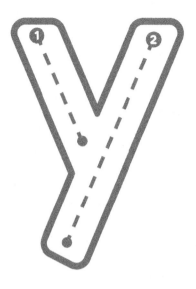
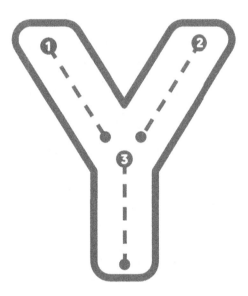
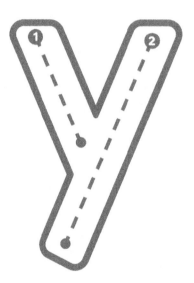
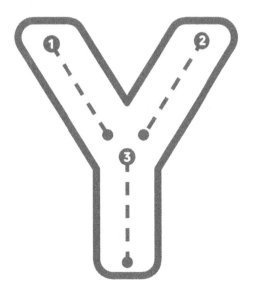
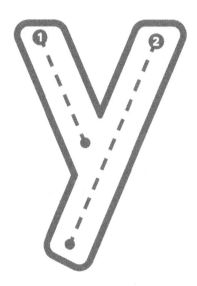

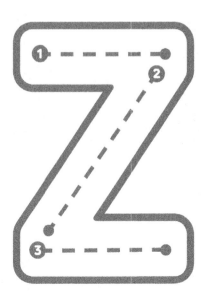

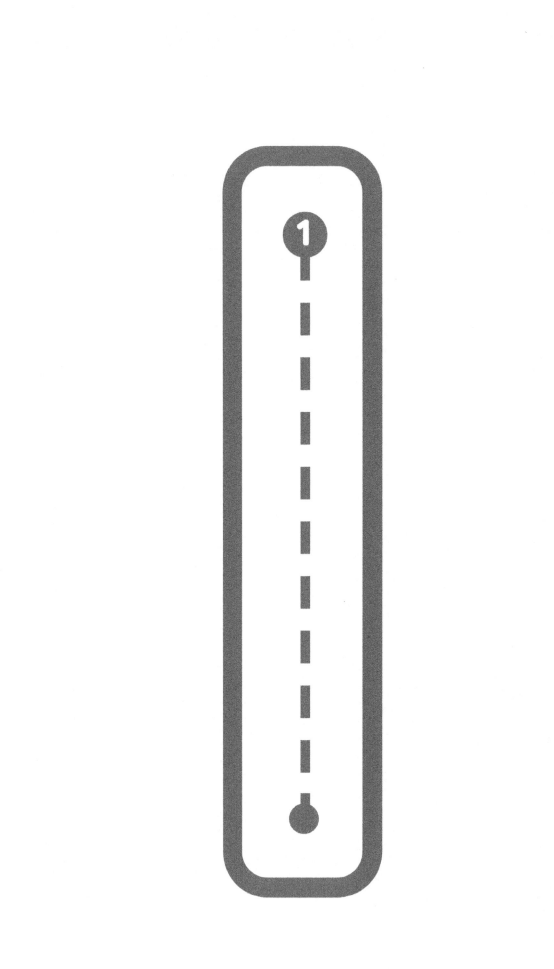

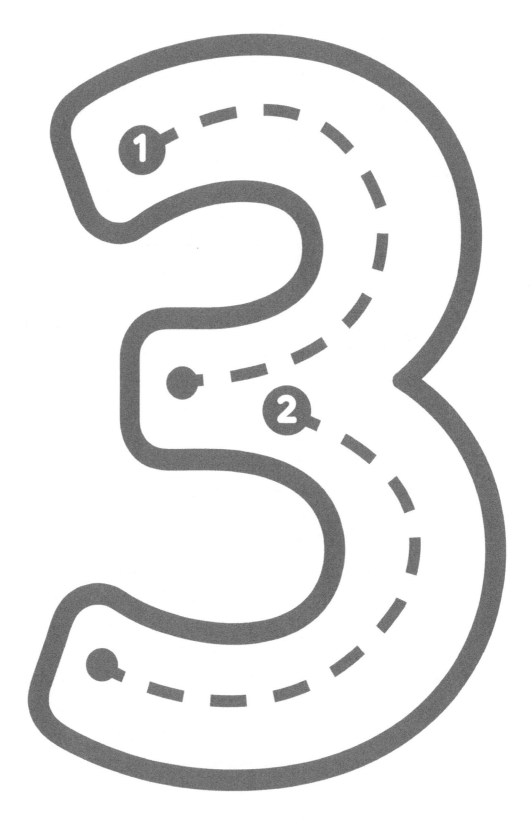

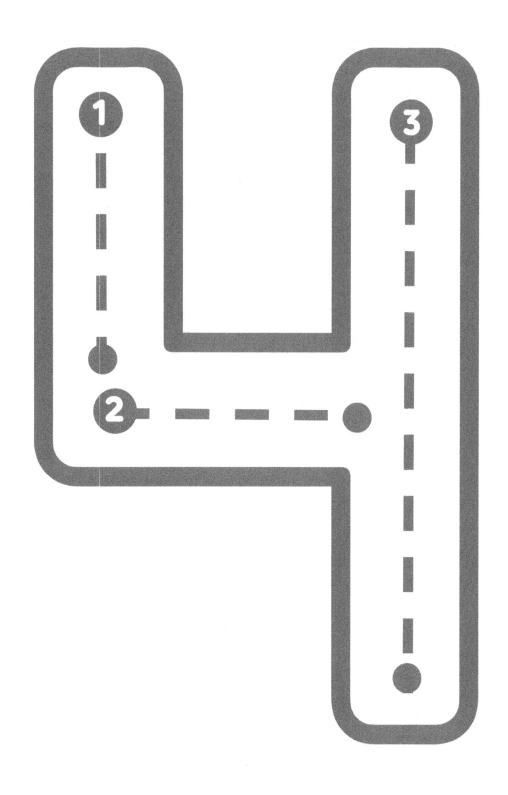

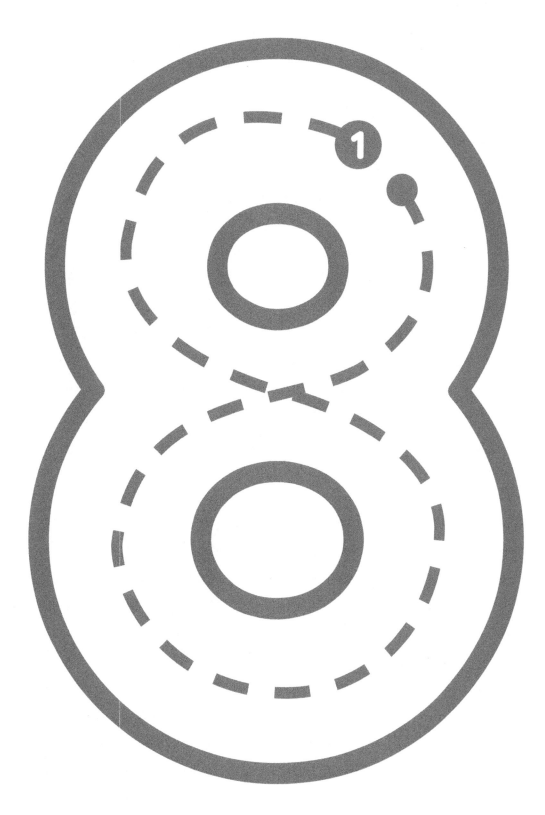

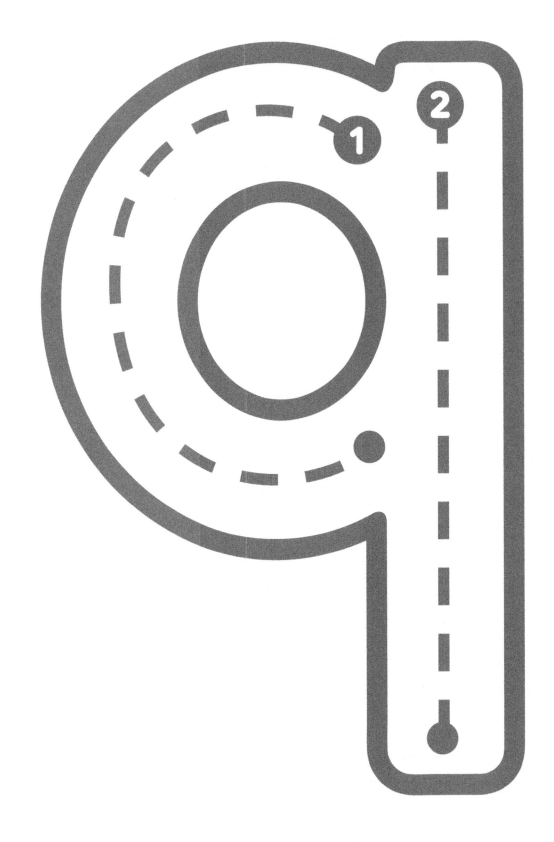

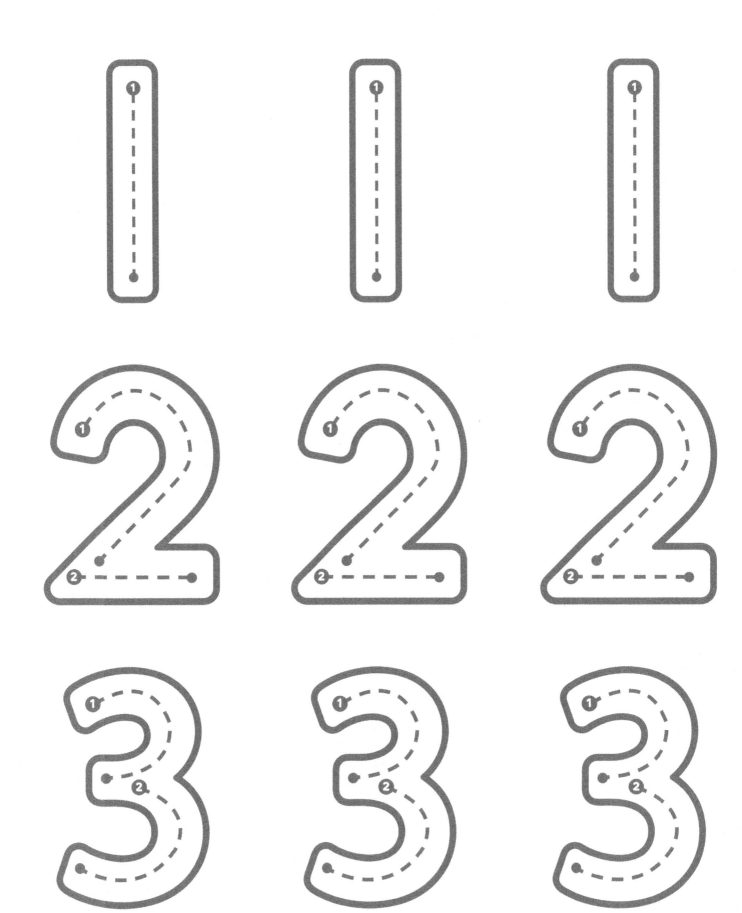

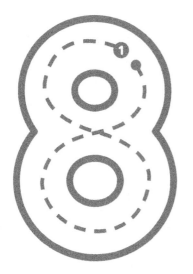 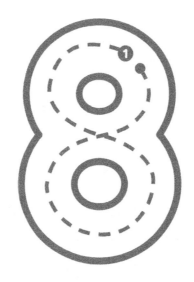 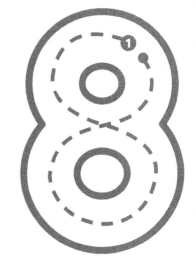

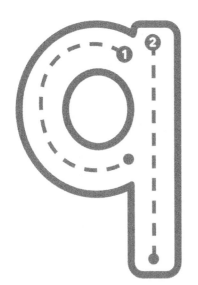 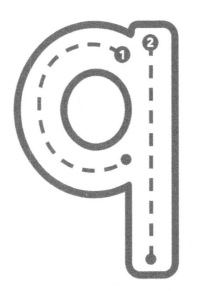 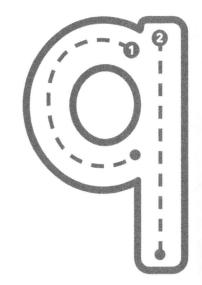

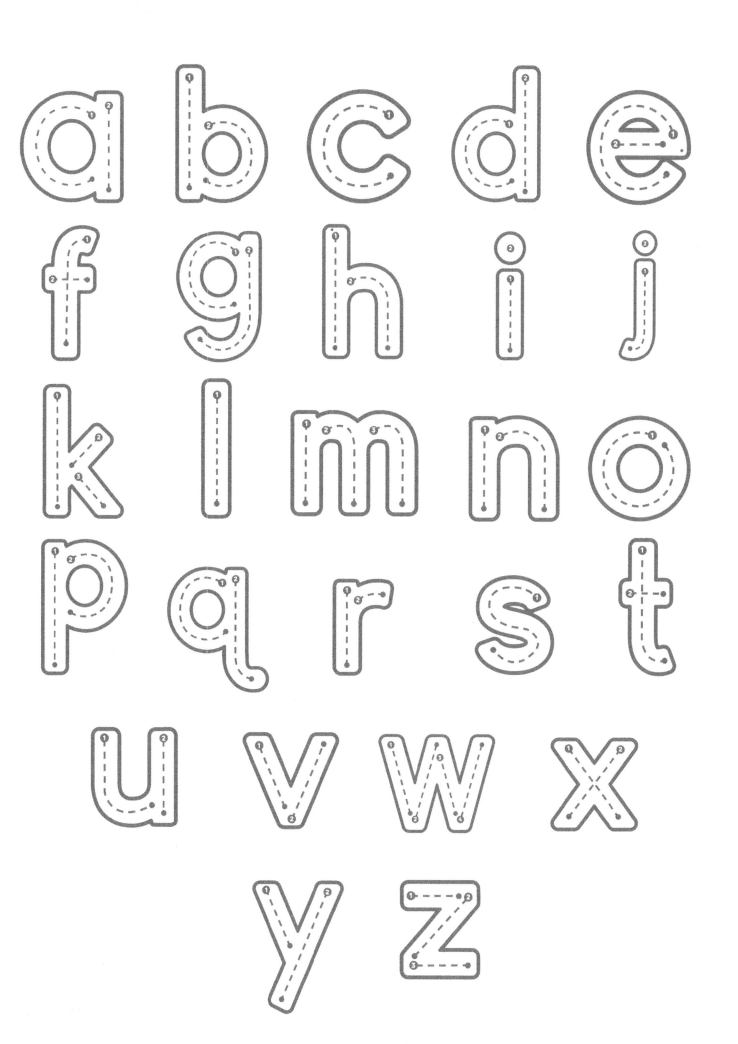

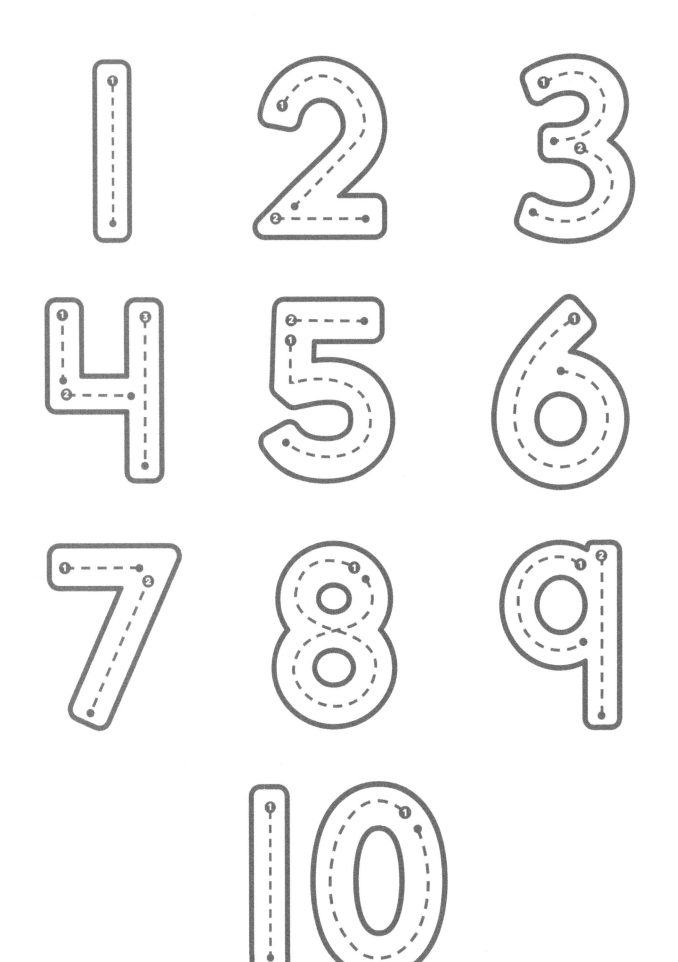

Certificate of
Achievement

Awarded to

_____

for excellence in

Big Letter Tracing Workbook

Date: _____

TOTALLY AWESOME

Signed _____

Hi !

My name is Anastasia Stephen. I am a mother of two toddlers. When my kids were growing up, I always wanted to enhance their writing skills and boost their creativity. This is the first book I made for my kids to trace, learn and develop the motor skills. Their progress was amazing, so i decided to publish it on Amazon.

This 8.5"x11" Big Workbook will help your child to enhance and develop the ability to grip the pencil. It has plenty of pages for hands-on practice. It will definitely prepare your child to excel in school.

I have included special easy guideline and directional arrows to assist your kid in writing. Your child will learn alphabets, numbers and shapes by the end of this book. I hope that you have liked my efforts in combining this book in the best possible manner.

Last but not the least, honest reviews from wonderful customers like you will help other parents feel confident about choosing this Big Letter Tracing book. I'd love to hear about your experience using this book. Feel free to send me your valuable suggestions I will be glad to incorporate it my upcoming children books.

I hope you enjoy the Big Letter Tracing Book!

Kind Regards,
Anastasia Stephen

https://anastasiastephen.com/

Made in United States
Orlando, FL
07 June 2023

33902782R00059